LETTERS TO SINGLE MOMS

RACHEL OCHIENG

Dedication

Thank you sweet Holy Spirit for you gave the Inspiration for these letters.

This book is dedicated to my daughter, Aisosa Ochieng, who trusted and believed in me as I constantly reminded her that we were a team of two and needed to work together, when deep down in my heart I was afraid of messing up a life entrusted to me. But God, in His infinite mercy saw us through.

And to my wonderful husband, God's very own gift to me, who came into our lives at the appointed time. Thank you for loving me and Sosa the way you do. Watching how you and Sosa get along melts my heart. In you, God gave me the full package. I love you.

This is also to all the single moms out there who are grinding really hard, who feel invisible. Sisters, I see you.

Table of Contents

Foreword

One of the most difficult things to do is to raise a child on your own. And yet in these times we find more and more people doing it.

In this book Rachel helps to outline some invaluable, helpful, and practical advice through her letters to you. Rachel shares how the Lord brought her through her own time of single parenting. As her pastor I witnessed Rachel apply these principles in her life and saw the blessings and results that came from her doing so. Rachel refused to compromise herself, her relationship with her daughter, and her walk with God. In her life you see the faithfulness of God prove true through the application of His Word.

I believe that these letters will bless you as you read them. God does not favor one over another so as He was faithful to Rachel, He will be with you.

Luis Rodriguez
Pastor of Full Life Christian Fellowship.
7 Brooklyn-Stanhope Rd, NJ 07874
Fulllifecf.org

Introduction

These letters are dedicated to single moms. I don't have the formula to retrace your steps and go back to the moment you weren't tasked with nursing, guiding and nurturing another human being. Those days of carefree living as you well know are gone. Responsibility is your new reality and that means you are misunderstood, judged and typecast as doing, thinking and acting a certain way. Despite the lonely nights, you keep fighting. Despite the uncertainty of the future you believe. Despite the financial struggles you stay in the moment and put one foot in front of the other. All you are gifted with is the present and your precious child or children to take care of. I've been there. I know how it feels so my hope is to shed light on the challenges you face. These are words of wisdom that were shared with me, and lessons I learned along the way as a single mom for 10 years. It is my hope that when you pick this up you feel loved, heard and understood. You are human, so it's time to take off that shell hiding your insecurities and it's time to take control of your life even when the world says you can't. The world does not know your story. Only you do. Discover the love of Jesus for yourself that is unfiltered and free from bias. Pick up your bible and let's journey together. These are my letters to single moms.

Letter One

I SEE YOU SIS

Dear Single Mom,

I see you grinding hard as you do the job of two. You are beautiful, bold and courageous. You are not a statistic. You are not your mistake. Who says your dream has to be completely over? You can begin to live again. You can believe in love again. You will find true love. Sister, I see you. You've got what it takes to raise not just a champion but champions. You are not ashamed to ask for help when needed. You are doing an excellent job. Sister dear, I see you. Jehovah Elroi sees you.   He is your strength.

Sister, remember Hagar whom the Lord literally placed the well at her feet when she could not see a way out to care for her son in the desert. See Genesis 21:19.

Letter Two

DEALING WITH LONELINESS

Dear Single Mom,

I understand your pain, I know what it feels like to go to bed every night wishing the one was there to keep you warm, yet you wonder if you can even be good enough for him. Let me tell you sister dear that you are good enough for THE ONE and do not settle for less. On those cold nights you can feel warm if you let the true and best lover love you while you wait for THE ONE that He will entrust you with. See, you are very valuable to Him so He wants to do His work in you first before He can hand you over to His chosen for you. So sister while you wait, will you whole heartedly serve?

Letter Three

FINANCIAL STRUGGLE

Dear Single Mom,

I see you stretching that dollar to the very last penny. You wonder how you are going to make ends meet again this month, wondering if those bills are ever going to get paid. I hear you sigh and ask if you will ever be able to get out of not ever having enough. Let me be the first to congratulate you sister dear, for you will come out of this. You will look back on this day and be thankful that you trusted in His word that said He will supply all of your needs according to His riches in glory by Christ Jesus.

Letter Four

FEELING LIKE A CHARITY CASE

Dear Single Mom,

Need I remind you that nobody can ever make you feel a certain type of way if you do not allow it. I know, I wish someone had told me this when I felt like a charity case every time someone wanted to do me a favor. Yes, sometimes, some people said hurtful things, but I had to ask Abba for wisdom to discern His real helpers among those who wanted to make me feel worse than I already felt. (Remember the Lord who sets the lonely in families,) who knows our every need, will bring the right people your way to help make this journey easy, you just have to trust and be open to what He   is doing.

"For as He thinketh in his heart, so is he…"

Proverbs 23:7 (KJV).

Letter Five

FORGIVENESS

Dear Single Mom,

Please whatever you do, regardless of the part you played in being on this journey, please be easy on yourself. Forgive yourself, and forgive the men involved. Do not hold on to grudges against anyone. Girl, you do not want to give anyone the power to control your life. The deed has been done; it's in the rear view mirror, so take responsibility for the part you played. Dust off your sandals, keep your chin up and get to work on creating a comfortable life for you and your child/children. Oh sister, how liberated you will feel.

Letter Six

FEAR FOR THE CHILDREN

Dear Single Mom,

Know that every parent, single or married, worries about their children, if they are doing the right thing. They worry about how they will turn out. Therefore, you are not out of line when you do worry or have those concerns. However, let me help ease your fear; take your worries to Abba, for He alone promises peace that the world cannot give. Besides, He has not given us the Spirit of fear. Once you come to a place of understanding that the Lord actually owns your children, and you have given them to Him, rest in knowing that you have kept them in the best hands and that they are safe.

"I will teach all your children, and they will enjoy great peace." Isaiah 54:13 (NLT).

Letter Seven

PRAYING FOR YOUR CHILD/CHILDREN

Dear Single Mom,

Pray, pray, pray often for your child/children as if your life depends on it (it really does). Your tongue has the power of life and death so choose to speak life over them regardless of what behavior they may be presenting. Celebrate every milestone and achievement with your child/children in whatever capacity you can, and watch your child/children flourish.

Letter Eight

Dear Single Mom,

This tie in with forgiveness. Never transfer your anger or frustration on your child/children and never see them as the reason for your challenges. Hey sis, you are the adult here, act like it. The worst thing you can do to a child/children's self-esteem is to constantly lash at them or talk them down because you are angry with the other parent. And please do not paint the other parent in a negative light either. Do your best to highlight the positives about the other parent, and let the child/children find out what else they need to find out for themselves when they are older. You do not want to sow a seed of discord in those child/children of yours, it might turn around to bite you, and they

might dislike you for it.

Letter Nine

TAKE A BREAK, PURSUE YOUR DREAMS

Dear Single Mom,

Please take a break if you need to. It's ok to get away and leave your child with a TRUSTED friend or family member. When you get some time away, you will come back refreshed and rejuvenated. You will be in a healthier mental state to care of your child/children. And sister dear, please do not believe that lie that your life is over. Get out that vision board, write down your plans and prayerfully pursue them trusting that God will bring you through one goal at a time.

Letter Ten

BLOCK YOUR EARS TO LIES

Dear Single Mom,

There is no other way to say this than to just say it! Sister dear, block your ears to the lies of the enemy that you are a statistic, or that your child/children fall into a certain category in society because of how they were born or because there is no father figure in their lives. Sister, trust me, God knows what you and your child/children need and He will make provisions if you can trust Him. Need I remind you that there are great men and women in our world that have turned out great regardless of being raised in a single parent home. All of these so-called statistics makes me wonder where and how the research is done!

Letter Eleven

FAMILY TIME

Dear Single Mom,

I'll let you in on a secret. When I was a single mom I felt a lot of guilt because I could not afford to give my daughter something she wanted or that I felt she could have. It was tough and because I have a child wiser that her age, I challenge her sometimes. During one of our quiet moments together, my daughter let me know that my time with her was more valuable than any material gift in the world. Oh sister, I took a deep breath that day, and felt like a load was lifted off my chest. I know you have to work. You may have to work two to three jobs, and sometimes you have classes because you are in school, but whatever you do, please make time for your child/children. Spend as much time with

them as much as you can.

Letter Twelve

GUILT-FREE LIVING

Dear Single Mom,

Let me share with you here what a wise godly woman once shared with me after observing my child when she spent time with her while I had to work. She said to never feel guilty because I'm the only parent in my child's life. Those children are extremely intelligent, and may want to use that against parents when they are being disciplined. In other words, she said not to be afraid or feel guilty when I have to discipline my child. Oh how I took this advice to heart. And it helped to raise a well behaved disciplined godly child. To God be the glory.

Letter Thirteen

RESPECT AND RELATIONSHIP

Dear Single Mom,

You know that saying that "if you demand respect, you have to first earn it," It couldn't be farther from the truth. As much as you want your child/children to respect you and themselves, you have to do likewise. You can talk from now till eternity and set rules, you model how you want your child/children to turn out. So I said this to say that, sister pertaining to dating, be sure to do it God's way. This way you avoid introducing your precious ones to multiple men. Dating God's way allows you to be prayerful, and with the help of your spiritual father, aka pastor, pick the right man. And please be sure to involve the child/children as they will be spending their whole life with this person. Do not spring some person on them and guilt them into accepting him. And sister, need I add that you do not have to settle because someone comes to make you feel they are doing you a favor by being married to you. Wait on God for His best, which will love all of you and treat you as the queen that you are.

Letter Fourteen

INVESTMENT AND MONEY MANAGEMENT

Dear Single Mom,

I know you might be thinking, shouldn't this have been under financial struggles? And yes, you are right to think that, but I am choosing to write a separate letter concerning this because of the importance I place on it, and I wish I was more disciplined in this area. You see, learning about how to manage your money frees you from all of those credit card debts. Yes, you heard me, credit card debts and yours truly had lots of them because in all honesty, they came handy. See I wasn't the type to be wasteful and spending foolishly, but I could have done better if I learned about investment and savings.

Thank God I am at a better place now after gradually paying off my debts. Hence my reason for sharing this with you. I am happy to have you learn from my mistakes. And be sure to set aside some savings for your children. There are a few college fund savings out there, look into the ones that would work for you, learn about them and begin to save. It doesn't have to be a huge amount. Just start. And do not be afraid to get your hands into several businesses. You just have to try until you hit that right one. When I was a single mom, I did explore a few business ideas and it felt good knowing that I had other sources of income other than my paid job. Sister dear, these are things I wish someone had shared with me. I am so passionate about sharing this with you. You will do yourself and your child/children a lot of good, and have more time to spend with them.

Letter Fifteen

FINAL NOTE

Dear Single Mom,

It has been my joy to somehow share my experience with you in hopes that you will be encouraged and continue to move ahead looking unto God the author and finisher of your faith, knowing that He sees you, and has a picture of you inscribed on the palm of His hand. He says in His word that He will never leave you or forsake you. Remember that in moments when you feel you cannot go on, The Lord's strength has you covered, for it is made perfect in your weakness. I thank you for taking time to write through these letters, and I look forward to hearing from you. Please do not hesitate to send me a reply. And if you have any questions, I will be honored to answer to the best of my ability. Or if you just need a listening ear, I will be here too, sister. Need I say it again, sister you are doing great. You ROCK!

And per adventure sister, you are reading this, you do not know the Lord Jesus Christ or have a relationship with Him, may I use this medium to invite you to open your heart to Him as He is knocking, and receive His grace & salvation. Please say this prayer with me; Dear Jesus, I come before you, a sinner, acknowledging you today as my Lord and Savior. I thank you for taking my place and dying on the cross. Thank you for the boldness to come before the Father because of your blood. Today I accept you as my Lord and Savior and I choose to follow where & how you lead me. Amen.

Blessings,

Rachel Ochieng.

All about the Author

Rachel Ochieng is the author of Grace in Adversity. She is known in her circle as a God chaser, because of her undying love for all that God represents. She is a licensed associate counselor in the State of New Jersey, and also a National Certified Counselor who has worked with individuals of all ages with mental health challenges. She is a wife of an excellent gentleman and a mother to two world changers. She is also a vlogger, and a blogger. She is passionate about helping people become their best. Her love for Christ fuels her love for people.